"A Year W

By
Gianna West

Dedication

This book is dedicated to my mom and my dad. They have helped me throughout my journey of working on my cookbook. I love them and I appreciate them for helping me through this project.

FORWARD

Working on this project has provided a healthy distraction for Gianna during hospital stays, doctor appointments, procedures, surgeries and constant pain. Every word is hers. Every recipe was tried and tested. Every picture was taken by her. This entire project was conceived and executed by a beautiful and kind-hearted girl who struggles so much yet has so much to give. "A Year With Gianna" is more than just a cookbook, it's a journey. A journey of hope. So, please, enter the journey and bon appetit.

Table of Contents

Biography..page 6

Appetizers
Asian-Greek Meatballs with Sweet and Spicy Sauce...........page 7
Baked Onion Rings with Tomato-Free Ketchup..................page 10
Bacon-Wrapped Stuffed Figs..page 13
Baked Stuffed Mushrooms...page 15
Cheesy Creamed Spinach with a Twist.............................page 17
Chopped Red Pepper Caprese Salad.................................page 20
Corn and Cauliflower Fritters..page 22
Deviled Eggs...page 24
Nana Coletti's Italian Bread..page 26
Nana Coletti's Stuffed Olives..page 28
Roasted Red Pepper Pico De Gallo..................................page 30
Root Beer Battered Stuffed Mushrooms...........................page 32
Shrimp and Cream Cheese Puffs.....................................page 34
Vegetarian Spring Rolls...page 36
Wasabi Deviled Eggs..page 38

Sauces and Soups
Alfredo Sauce..page 67
Honey Mustard Sauce... page 124
Mock Guacamole...page 40
Not Thousand Island Salad Dressing..............................page 42
Pepper Marinara..page 44
Spicy Honey Mustard Sauce..page 55
Sweet and Spicy Sauce...page 7
Tomato-Free Ketchup...page 11

Entrees
Bacon-Wrapped Cheese Dogs..page 46
Baked Macaroni and Cheese...page 48
Barbeque Beef Baby Back Ribs.....................................page 50
Beef Pockets..page 52
Breaded Stuffed Chicken Breasts with
   Spicy Honey Mustard Sauce...................................page 54
Cheesy Meaty Nachos...page 56
Chicken Ravioli..page 58

Chicken Kabobs and Vegetable Kabobs................................,,,,,.page 61
Chicken Pinwheels...page 63
Deep Fried Smoked Salmon and Cream Cheese Wontons..........page 65
Egg Noodle Dough...page 86
Gianna's Shrimp Alfredo...page 67

Gouda-Stuffed Hamburgers...page 69
Italian Stuffed Red Peppers... page 71
Loaded Chicken and Potatoes..page 73
Nutty Korean Chicken Tenders..page 75
Oyster and Clam Chowder...page 77
Roasted Red Pepper and Goat Cheese Soup................................page 79
Spicy Shrimp Salad..page 82
Spicy Baked Scottish Eggs...page 84
Spinach, Ricotta, and Shrimp Lasagna...page 86
Sweet Italian Sausage and Three Cheese Ravioli........................page 88
White Pizza with Spicy Capri Cola, Green Peppers,
   Mozzarella, and Black Olives..page 90

Side Dishes
Cucumber Salad...page 94
Garlic and Shrimp Twice-Baked Potatoes...................................page 96
Potato Salad...page 98
Sweet Potato Fries...page 100
Tomato-Free Baked Beans..page 102

Desserts
Mini Blueberry Shortcakes..page 104
Peanutty Chocolaty Pies..page 106
Spicy Chocolate Cupcakes with Chocolate Cream
   Cheese Frosting ....page 108
Refrigerator Cake..page 111
Vegan Peanut Butter and Nut Balls...page 113
White Chocolate Peanut Butter Fudge..page 115

Signature Burgers
The Big Daddy Burger...page 117
The Gianna Surprise..page 119

The Grandma Dora Sandwich..page 121
The Grandpa Phil Burger..page 123
The Momma Linda Burger...page 125
The Rock Star Burger...page 127

Restaurant Reviews
Field Stone Grill (Portage, MI)..page 129
Five Guys Burgers and Fries (chain).......................................page 130
Hibachi Restaurant and Grill (Matteson, IL).........................page 131
Hyde Park Market Place (Chicago, IL)...................................page 132

Longhorn Steakhouse (chain)...page 133
Max and Benny's Restaurant, Bakery and Deli
    (Northbrook, IL)...page 134
Mimi's Cafe (chain)..page 135
Oma's Restaurant (Frankenmuth, MI)...................................page 136

Cooking Challenges
(explanation and sample)..page 137

Biography

Hi, my name is Gianna West and I am a 15 year-old girl with spina bifida, a disability that can affect your body. Spina bifida has affected the left side of my body pretty badly so I have limited use of my left hand. Sometimes it can stop me from doing things, but it will never stop me from doing what I love the most: cooking. I have always had a passion for cooking ever since I was a young girl. My passion for cooking came from my dad. A lot of the time when he is in the kitchen making something, I would go in there and help him. Also, I always watch cooking shows when I have a chance. I have always wanted to be a chef when I grow up. I decided that I wanted to do culinary arts as an elective for school. I wanted to work on a cookbook which is latex-free which means there are no tomatoes, avocados, bananas, water chestnuts(which I do not like anyways). It also means that I cannot handle raw white potatoes. I even decided to take a substitution for tomatoes and avocados and figure out a way to make marinara sauce and guacamole. I know it sounds weird but it really works. I even have some of my parents' favorite recipes in here. I have a section in here that is called "West Family Signature Burgers" which has burgers that represent me, my brother, my mom, my dad, my grandpa, and my grandma. I hope you enjoy " A Year with Gianna".

Appetizers

Asian-Greek Meatballs with Sweet and Spicy Sauce

I made this recipe because I wanted to make my own version of meatballs because it is one of my favorite Italian dishes. This recipe is made with 3 types of meat. This can be paired with my Pepper Marinara, Homemade Alfredo sauce, my Tomato-Free Ketchup, or my Sweet and Spicy sauce. This recipe can be used at parties. This recipe is absolutely to die for.

Ingredients:

Sweet and Spicy sauce:

1 cup mayonnaise

1 cup Tomato-Free Ketchup (see recipe page 11)

2 tablespoons yellow mustard

1 teaspoon ground red pepper

1 tablespoon black pepper

1 teaspoon salt

1 tablespoon grated asiago cheese

1 ½ tablespoons white sugar

Meatballs:

½ pound chopped sirloin

½ pound ground lamb

½ pound ground pork

2 cups grated parmesan cheese

1/3 cup feta cheese

½ block garlic and herb flavored goat cheese

1 cup breadcrumbs

1 egg

1 tablespoon sesame seed oil

1 tablespoon soy sauce

1 tablespoon worcestershire sauce

1 teaspoon salt

1 teaspoon pepper

1 teaspoon ground red pepper

Directions:

1. For the sauce, mix the mayonnaise, ketchup, mustard, cheese, black pepper, red pepper, salt, and sugar in a small bowl and refrigerate until ready to serve.
2. Mix the meat, cheeses, and seasonings in a bowl
3. Form into golf-ball size balls
4. Place on a cookie sheet lined with foil
5. Cook in a 425 degree oven for 25 minutes
6. Remove and let cool
7. Serve with sauce
8. Enjoy!

Baked Onion Rings with Tomato-Free Ketchup

This recipe was one that I came up with because I wanted to make a healthier version of the original fried onion rings. I baked these onions instead of deep-frying them. My ketchup recipe has no tomatoes because I cannot have tomatoes but it does have cranberry sauce in it. Both of these recipes are so good.

Ingredients:

Onion Rings:

½ of a large red onion, separate rings

½ of a small bag of panko breadcrumbs

½ a bottle of buttermilk

3 splashes of worcestershire sauce

¼ cup brown sugar

¼ cup grated Parmesan cheese

1 tablespoon salt

1 tablespoon pepper

Tomato-Free Ketchup:

    1(16 ounce) can jellied cranberry sauce

    1(16 ounce) can pear halves in natural juice, drained

    1(16 ounce) can sliced carrots, drained

    ½ cup white vinegar

    ¼ cup granulated sugar(you do not have to add it if you do not like it too sweet)

    ¼ cup white corn syrup (Karo)

    4 teaspoons salt

    1 teaspoon pepper

    1 teaspoon onion powder

    ¼ teaspoon allspice

    1/8 teaspoon ground cloves

Directions:

1. To make the ketchup use the blender to process the ingredients until smooth. About 30 seconds
2. Store in refrigerator
3. Add the flour, salt, and pepper to one bowl
4. Add the worcestershire sauce to the buttermilk in another bowl
5. Put the breadcrumbs, brown sugar, and parmesan cheese to another bowl

6. Dredge the onions in the buttermilk, flour, back into the buttermilk, and then into the breadcrumbs.

7. Bake at 400 degrees for 15 minutes

8. Take out and let cool

9. Serve and enjoy!

Bacon-Wrapped Stuffed Figs

This is a recipe I came up with because we had a lot of figs in our house which our neighbor gave us. I used a lot of cheese and seasonings. I like figs so I decided to do this and it worked. This recipe dish is fatty but who cares? You can use this recipe for a party or just as a snack for yourself.

Ingredients:

1 pint black mission figs, halved and hollowed

1/3 cup feta cheese

1 cup ricotta cheese

½ cup parmesan cheese

1 teaspoon salt

2 teaspoons black pepper

1 tablespoon garlic powder

1 tablespoon white sugar

6 slabs of bacon, cut in half

Directions:

1. Take the figs and wash them thoroughly

2. Cut the tips off the figs then cut them in half

3. Hollow out the figs and throw out the insides

4. Mix the feta cheese, ricotta cheese, parmesan cheese, garlic powder, salt, pepper, and sugar in a small bowl

5. Add a little bit of the filling and fill each fig half

6. Wrap each fig in a piece of bacon and roll it up

7. Put the figs on a cookie sheet with foil on it. Spray the foil before you place the figs on it.

8. Place in a 400 degree oven for 22 minutes until bacon is crispy

9. Remove from oven and place on a plate lined with paper towels

10. Serve and enjoy!

Baked Stuffed Mushrooms

This is a recipe that my dad made for when we went to a friend's house. This recipe is perfect for a party or just to share as a family. This recipe is very simple and delicious. This recipe is similar to my own mushroom recipe, but we changed it up a little.

Ingredients:

1 package frozen spinach , thawed (you can use fresh if you want)

1 package button mushrooms

1 ½ cups ricotta cheese

cayenne pepper, to taste

salt, to taste

pepper, to taste

garlic powder, to taste

1 cup breadcrumbs

½ cup parmesan cheese

Directions:

1. Wash the mushrooms thoroughly and remove the stems
2. Mix the ricotta, spinach, cayenne, salt, pepper, and garlic powder in a large bowl
3. Fill the mushrooms with about a tablespoon of the filling(do not over stuff them)
4. Add the breadcrumb and cheese mixture
5. Bake in a 375 degree oven for about 20 minutes
6. Remove from oven and let cool
7. Serve and enjoy

Cheesy Creamed Spinach with a Twist

I came up with this recipe because I wanted to make something that was sort of unusual. Like the average creamed spinach, this is creamy and healthy(not). I decided to use sausage in this to give it a different flavor and a uniqueness. Everything in this recipe is fresh. You can make this for any occasion or just for a regular family meal. This recipe is so good that it makes you feel relaxed when you eat it.

Ingredients:

9oz tender spinach, washed(any kind of spinach works too)

1 pound sweet Italian sausage

½ 8 oz tub Centrella cream cheese

1½ cups shredded mozzarella cheese

1 ½ cups grated parmesan cheese

¼ teaspoon black pepper

2 teaspoons ground red pepper(cayenne)

1 tablespoon onion powder

2 pinches salt

2 Tablespoons whole grain mustard

1 tablespoon minced garlic

2 teaspoons sugar

2 splashes of milk

½ teaspoon dried oregano

Directions:

1. Wash the spinach first(if not already pre-washed).
2. Cook in a medium pan until completely cooked. Cook in about a tablespoon of olive oil on medium heat.
3. Then cook sausage in same pan in olive oil until slightly pink(it will finish in the oven. 4. Cook on medium heat.
5. Mix the spinach, sausage, cream cheese, ½ cup mozzarella cheese, ½ cup parmesan cheese, black pepper, red pepper, onion powder, salt, mustard, minced garlic, sugar, oregano, and milk in a small bowl.
6. Add mixture to a medium-sized pan that is sprayed. Spread out evenly.

7. Add the 1 cup of mozzarella cheese and the 1 cup of parmesan cheese.

8. Bake in a 350 degree oven for 20 minutes.

9. Remove from oven and let cool.

10. Serve with crackers or French or Italian bread.

11. Enjoy!

Chopped Red Pepper Caprese Salad

I came up with this recipe because I love the traditional Caprese salad but I cannot have tomatoes so I decided that I wanted to recreate this salad. This recipe has some crunch to it and it is also tangy from the balsamic vinegar. This recipe can be used for parties or just a regular side dish for a dinner. Since I didn't have regular Italian basil I had to use Thai basil.

Ingredients:

2 red bell peppers, roasted and seeded

1 cup of balsamic vinegar

½ cup olive oil

1 tablespoon chopped fresh Thai basil

1 ½ blocks fresh mozzarella cheese, cut into cubes

1 pinch kosher salt

1 teaspoon pepper

Directions:

1. Roast the peppers on a sheet pan lined with aluminum foil for 20 minutes in a 400 degree oven. Drizzle with olive oil first.
2. Cut into small pieces
3. Mix all the ingredients in a small bowl
4. Serve with a baguette or chips and enjoy!

Corn and Cauliflower Fritters

This is a recipe that my mom came up with because we had leftover cauliflower. My mom also used canned corn in this recipe (if you want just use fresh corn). This is so decadent and delicious and also its healthy..sort of. This recipe is perfect for a party or just a family dinner.

Ingredients:

2 cups cauliflower, cooked and smashed

3 whole eggs

2 tablespoons garlic powder

½ teaspoon salt

1 teaspoon black pepper

1 can of corn, drained

2 teaspoons chopped green onions

flour as needed

Directions:

1. Mix all the ingredients in a large bowl. Cook the cauliflower first
2. Form into golf ball size balls
3. Cook in a pan with oil on medium heat for 2 minutes on each side
4. Remove a place fritters on a plate lined with a paper towel
5. Serve and enjoy!

Deviled Eggs

My family and I made these deviled eggs for 4th of July one year as an appetizer. We kept it traditional but that was all we needed. These eggs are creamy and delicious. It is also very simple to make, so you can make these ahead of time if you want. You can also put your own twist on it to make it your own.

Ingredients:

6 eggs, boiled and peeled and halved

2 tablespoon mayonnaise(you can always add more if needed)

mustard to taste

1 teaspoon salt

1 teaspoon black pepper

dill to taste

Directions:

1. Boil the eggs for about 10-12 minutes and peel

2. Mix the yolks, salt, pepper, dill, mustard, and mayonnaise until smooth

3. Put about a tablespoon of the filling into each egg half

4. Top with dill and smoked paprika

5. Refrigerate until ready to serve.

6. Enjoy!

Nana Coletti's Italian Bread

My family's recipe for Italian Bread was passed down from my great-grandmother to my grandmother to my mom down to me. This recipe has been a favorite in my family for years because it has the perfect balance of flavors. This process takes a while but it is worth the wait because it is so warm and flaky. This recipe is good for sandwiches and it is also great with just butter.

Ingredients:

5 pounds of white flour

3 eggs

3 packages dry yeast, dissolved in 1 cup of hot water

1 stick butter or margarine, melted

palmful of salt

1 cup milk

1 small kettleful of hot water

Directions:

1. Flour in stock pot

2. Make well in middle

3. Add eggs, yeast, butter, salt, and milk

4. Start mixing slowly adding hot water until you get a doughy consistency. You do not want it too wet,

5. Knead well

6. Cover and let rise for two hours

7. Knead again and form loaves, (We make braided loaves)

8. Put dough in loaf pans and let rise for another two hours

9. Bake at 350 degrees for 30 minutes

10. Remove loaves from pans

11. Put loaves on oven rack and bake another 20 minutes until golden brown

12. Let cool and enjoy!

Nana Coletti's Stuffed Olives

My family's recipe for stuffed olives is a family favorite because it is packed with flavor. This recipe has been in my family for three generations. This is one of my favorite recipes because it is salty and crunchy and deep-fried which makes it so delicious.

Ingredients:

2 jars large Spanish olives

2 pounds ground beef

1/8 cup fresh parsley

2 cloves garlic, minced

1 pinch of salt

2 pinches of black pepper

2 cups flour

4-6 eggs

2 cups breadcrumbs

1/4 cup olive oil

Directions:

1. Using pairing knife cut olive off of pit in a spiral (This takes practice don't despair). Save juice from one jar.

2. In large bowl mix meat, olive juice, parsley salt, pepper, garlic, and one egg.

3. Make little meatballs

4. Wrap olive around little meatball, giving it a squeeze

5. Continue until all meatballs are gone.

6. Cover and refrigerate overnight

7. Roll olives in flour, eggs, and breadcrumbs

8. Deep-fry until golden brown

9. Drain on paper towels

10. Serve and enjoy!

Roasted Red Pepper Pico De Gallo

I came up with this recipe because I wanted to make an alternative to the traditional pico de gallo, since I am allergic to tomatoes. This dish is kind of spicy because I used a jalapeno. This is also very healthy for people and it is very fast to make.

Ingredients:

2 red bell peppers, roasted and seeded

1 small yellow onion, chopped

1 jalapeno, seeds and membrane removed

1 pinch kosher salt

1 teaspoon black pepper

1 tablespoon fresh cilantro

Juice of one small lime

Directions:

1. Roast the peppers in the oven on a sheet pan lined with aluminum foil. Drizzle with olive oil first. Roast in a 400 degree oven for 20 minutes.
2. Remove from oven and remove skin
3. Cut the peppers into small bite-size pieces
4. Mix the peppers, cilantro, chopped jalapeno, lime juice, salt, pepper, and onion in a small bowl.
5. Serve with chips and enjoy!

Root Beer Battered Stuffed Mushrooms

This recipe is something that I came up with because I love stuffed mushrooms so I decided to come up with my own recipe. You can stuff these with anything but I chose to use cheese and spinach. This recipe took some effort but I finally got it right.

Ingredients:

10 ounces frozen spinach (use fresh if possible if you like)

1(8 oz) block cream cheese

1 (12 oz) can root beer soda

1 package button mushrooms

2 cups all-purpose flour

1 teaspoon cayenne pepper

½ teaspoon baking powder

Directions:

1. Wash the mushrooms until clean
2. Remove the stems from the mushrooms
3. Mix the cheese and spinach in small bowl
4. Stuff the mushrooms with the spinach and cream cheese mixture
5. Coat the mushrooms in the batter
6. Fry the mushrooms in a 2 quart pot filled halfway with vegetable oil just enough to cover the mushrooms.
7. Let drain on a plate lined with a paper towel
8. Serve with The Not Thousand Island Salad Dressing(see recipe on page 42)
9. Eat and enjoy!

Shrimp and Cream Cheese Puffs

This is a recipe that I thought of because I like shrimp and cheese. I wanted to create a version of the crab rangoon that can be found at most Chinese restaurants. These puffs are nice and flaky and delicious. This recipe takes patience because this is difficult to make, but that is okay, you just need to practice .

Ingredients:

1(8oz) package cream cheese

1 tablespoon black pepper

1 tablespoon smoked paprika

1 tablespoon cayenne pepper

1 teaspoon salt

½ cup Parmesan cheese

2 cups shrimp, cooked and chopped(tails removed)

4 sheets phyllo dough

¼ cup green onions,cut

1 egg

Directions:

1. Cut the shrimp after removing the tails
2. Mix the shrimp, green onions(cut thinly with scissors), salt, pepper, cayenne, smoked paprika, and Parmesan cheese in a large bowl
3. lay a sheet of dough onto the cookie sheet lined with foil and egg wash it completely
4. Add another layer and egg was that
5. Add about a tablespoon of the filling about ½ inch apart
6. Add two more layers of phyllo dough
7. Egg wash the top
8. Put in oven at 300 degrees for 15 minutes or until brown
9. Remove from the oven and let cool
10. Serve with ant dipping sauce you want
11. Enjoy!

Vegetarian Spring Rolls

Even though I am not a vegetarian, I wanted to make a different version of the classic spring roll. This recipe is light and delicious. This would be a good appetizer for parties or even just for a family. The spring roll wrappers are hard to handle but you will eventually get used to it, I promise. This originally makes 5 rolls but you can make as many as you like.

Ingredients:

5 spring roll wrappers

1 can navy beans, drained

1 small container cream cheese

1 handful Italian or plain parsley, snipped

1 handful fresh basil, snipped

¼ teaspoon salt

½ teaspoon black pepper

1 teaspoon onion powder

3 teaspoons white sugar

1 tablespoon low sodium soy sauce

Directions:

1. Soak spring roll wrappers for 10 seconds. Let dry on a towel for 30 seconds
2. Mix the beans (drain and smash first), cream cheese, parsley, basil, soy sauce, salt, pepper, onion powder, and sugar in a small bowl.
3. Place on a sheet pan lined with aluminum foil
4. Bake in a 400 degree oven for 25 minutes
5. Remove from oven and let cool
6. Serve and enjoy

Wasabi Deviled Eggs

This is a recipe that my dad made on Father's Day to go with our dinner. This recipe is very simple and delicious. My dad decided to make it spicy by using wasabi sauce. This recipe is creamy and absolutely perfect thanks to my dad, who is a great cook.

Ingredients:

12 eggs, halved

1 tablespoon French's yellow mustard

1 tablespoon wasabi sauce

½ teaspoon black pepper

½ teaspoon salt

1 teaspoon dill

Directions:

1. Boil the eggs for 10 minutes in a small pan with water

2. Peel the eggs and scoop out the filling

3. Mix the eggs, mustard, wasabi, salt, pepper, and dill in a small bowl

4. Scoop about a tablespoon or so of the mixture into each half

5. Garnish with extra dill and smoked paprika

6. Serve and enjoy!

Sauces and Soups

Mock Guacamole

This recipe is something that I came up as a substitute for regular guacamole. Since I cannot have avocados, I used asparagus. This dish has many layers of flavors from the chips to the cilantro. You can serve this with nachos, like I did, or just serve it with tortilla chips for dipping.

Ingredients:

8 ounces asparagus (34-36 skinny spears, ends trimmed)

1 cup plus 2 tablespoons peas (fresh or frozen is just fine)

2 tablespoons mayonnaise or miracle whip

Juice of ½ a lime

1 ½ tsp minced garlic

½ tsp cumin

1/4 tsp salt

½ teaspoon pepper

2 tablespoons diced red onion

optional: 2 teaspoons dry cilantro

optional: sweetener (regular sugar or Splenda)

Directions: 1. Steam the asparagus just until soft, then combine all ingredients(except onion) and blend in food processor until very smooth.

2. Stir in onion (you can omit if desired).

3. Refrigerate until cold. (or you can steam the asparagus in advance and chill them, so your dip will be cold after blending.)

Not Thousand Island Salad Dressing

This recipe is an alternative to the original Thousand Island Dression because there is no ketchup in it. This is perfect for parties and get-to-gethers. My friend found this recipe online but I made changes to it to make it my own. This recipe is absolutely to die for because it is so good. If you are having a party with a big crowd, you can always double the recipe.

Illustration: Shown here with Root Beer Stuffed Mushrooms

Ingredients:

½ cup real mayonnaise

½ teaspoon paprika

1 teaspoon white vinegar

1/8- ¼ teaspoon stevia or regular white sugar

enough filtered water to meet your desired consistency

Directions:

1. Whisk together above ingredients in a small container until all lumps are smooth.

2. Add the water a little bit at a time to meet the thickness or thinness you desire.

3. Serve and enjoy!

Pepper Marinara

I decided to create an alternative to traditional marinara sauce and call Pepper Marinara. I used red bell peppers instead of tomatoes because I have a latex allergy and I cannot have tomatoes. After I found the right flavors and consistency for this recipe, I used it for a few other dishes that I have created. This recipe can be used for dipping, lasagna, spaghetti and pizza sauces. This recipe is to die for because it is delicious and easy to make.

Ingredients:

2 large red bell peppers, seeded and cut

2 tablespoons of balsamic vinegar

2-3 teaspoons of garlic powder or minced garlic

2 teaspoons of salt

2 teaspoons of pepper

3 teaspoons of oregano

1-2 tablespoons of white sugar

2 tablespoons of dried or fresh basil

Directions: 1. Cut the two large red bell peppers to get the seeds and membranes out.

2. Saute the peppers in a medium pan with olive oil until they are soft(5-10 Minutes).

3. Put the peppers into a food processor and blend until there are no leftover pieces.

4. Add seasonings then blend again.

5. Cook down the sauce for 10 minutes.

6. Put in large bowl then refrigerate until ready to use.

Entrees

Bacon-Wrapped Cheese Dogs

My dad's recipe for Bacon Wrapped Cheese Dogs is a mouth-watering recipe that is packed full of flavor. You can put anything on this hot dog: onions, cheese, jalapenos, mustard, or anything you might imagine.

Ingredients:

1 pack of beef hotdogs

4-5 slabs of bacon

1 cup white onions

3 slices of fresh Mozzarella (any kind of cheese will be fine

1 squirt of mustard (or any other toppings you would like)

Directions:

1. Take the hotdogs and wrap them in a piece of bacon

2. Take a small or medium saucepan and melt a tablespoon of butter

3. Saute the onions in the pan for 5-10 minutes or until soft

4. Cook the hotdogs until the bacon is crispy.

5. Assemble the hot dogs and top them with any ingredients you like.

6. Serve and enjoy!

Baked Macaroni and Cheese

This is a recipe that I came up with because I really love macaroni and cheese. I used cheeses that are not normally used in this dish. This recipe is so gooey and delicious. I was going to put bacon in it but I tasted it and I decided this recipe did not need bacon. This recipe is good for parties and picnics. It is very comforting on hot days or any other day.

Ingredients:

1 ¾ cup 2% milk

¼ cup flour

½ cup (one stick) unsalted butter

1 cup grated asiago cheese

1 box cavatappi pasta

½ block gorgonzola cheese

½ block brie cheese

2 teaspoons salt

2 teaspoons black pepper

2 teaspoons ground red pepper

1 cup breadcrumbs(Italian or regular)

1 cup Parmesan cheese

Directions:

1. Add the butter and flour in a medium-sized pan to make a roux. Add the milk with the pan off The heat.
2. Add the cheese and stir until melted on low heat
3. Cook the pasta in boiling water until the pasta is cooked. Drain the pasta.
4. Add the pasta to the cheese sauce and stir
5. Put into a pan and cook at 400 degrees for fifteen minutes
6. Remove from oven and let cool
7. Serve and enjoy!

Barbeque Beef Baby Back Ribs

My family and I made these ribs as an entree for 4th of July to go along with our deviled eggs. We used two styles of barbecue sauce: Traditional and Korean (which has no tomatoes). These take a little while to make but, let me tell you, it is so worth the work.

Ingredients:

3 racks Beef Baby back ribs

Korean barbeque sauce of your choice (for those with latex allergies)

salt and pepper

onion powder

garlic powder

smoked paprika

Directions:

1. Season the ribs after you take the extra fat off them
2. Precook the ribs in the oven for about an hour
3. Cook on the grill About 10-12 minutes on each side
4. Brush with the barbeque sauce
5. Remove from grill and let cool
6. Cover with more sauce if desired
7. Serve and enjoy

Beef Pockets

My dad's recipe for Beef Pockets is absolutely delicious because it is cheesy and crispy. This recipe is succulent and absolutely easy to make. You can put anything in here with the meat like onions and cheese or whatever you like.

Ingredients:

2 packs Pillsbury Grand Biscuit Dough

1 1/2 pounds ground beef, cooked

1 teaspoon salt

1 teaspoon pepper

1 teaspoon garlic powder

1 onion, chopped and sauteed

shredded mozzarella cheese or cheese blend, any kind will work just fine

oregano

Directions:

1. Cook ground beef and onions in separate pans and season meat with salt, pepper, and garlic powder.

2. Flatten biscuits very thin (about 1/2 inch thick)

3. Fill dough with the meat, onions, and the cheese

4. Fold over and seal well

5. Cook at 350 degrees for 13-17 minutes

6. Take out of the oven and let cool

7. Cut open and enjoy!

Breaded Stuffed Chicken Breasts with Spicy Honey Mustard Sauce

I came up with this recipe because I love chicken breasts and I wanted to do something different with them. This recipe is so good and comforting and the sauce compliments this chicken very well. If you have a big party you can always double the recipe.

Ingredients:

Chicken:

4-5 frozen boneless chicken breasts, thawed (please use fresh if you can)

½ cup regular breadcrumbs

½ cup oatmeal

¼ cup parmesan cheese

2 eggs

½ teaspoon salt

1 teaspoon black pepper

¼ teaspoon dried oregano

1/8 teaspoon dried basil

½ cup butter

Spicy Honey Mustard Sauce:

¼ cup mayonnaise

2 tablespoon yellow mustard

1/8 teaspoon cayenne

4 tablespoons honey

Directions:

1. Mix the butter, salt, pepper, oregano, and basil in a food processor.
2. Take the chicken and make a little slit across the middle. Stuff some of the butter in the pocket. Add a little salt and oregano on top.
3. Take two bowls add two eggs to one bowl and the breadcrumb, oatmeal, and parmesan cheese mixture to another bowl.
4. Place on a cookie sheet lined with foil.
5. Bake in a 375 degree oven for 45 minutes.
6. Take it out of the oven and let cool.
7. Take a small bowl and mix the mayonnaise, mustard, honey, and cayenne.
8. Serve with the chicken and enjoy!

Cheesy Meaty Nachos

I decided to make these nachos because it is one of my favorite Mexican dishes. These nachos are so cheesy and delicious. These nachos can be made on any day of the week for breakfast, lunch or dinner. You can also make this dish the night before and put it into the refrigerator overnight.

Ingredients:

½ of a large bag of tortilla chips

½ a bag of shredded cheese blend (chedder and kolby jack) and crumbled cheese

sour cream (for the top)

green onions

½ pound of ground beef

1 can re-fried beans

Mock Guacamole (see recipe page 40)

Directions:

1. Gather ingredients
2. Brown the beef
3. Layer chips in medium baking dish
4. Layer the beef, refried beans, and cheese
5. Cook in broiler for three minutes to melt the cheese
6. Serve with sour cream, green onions, Mock Guacamole, and jalapenos.
7. Eat and enjoy!

Chicken Ravioli

(Shown here with Pepper Marinara sauce)

Our family's recipe for Chicken Ravioli was passed down from my great-grandmother to my grandma to my mom and (now) to me. This recipe takes two days to make but it is absolutely to die for because it is packed with flavor.

Filling:

Ingredients:

    1 stewing hen

    1 stalk celery

    1 carrot

    1 handful fresh parsley

    a quarter of an onion

1 teaspoon salt

1/2 teaspoon pepper

1/2 a loaf Italian bread, torn into chunks

3 eggs, beaten

1/2 cup lemon juice

grated rind of one lemon

1 cup sugar

1 teaspoon cinnamon

1 teaspoon nutmeg

1/2 teaspoon poultry seasoning

Directions:

1. Put stewing hen, carrot, celery, onion, parsley, salt and pepper in stock pot. Cover with water. Bring to boil then let simmer for four hours. Skim fat off the top.
2. Remove chicken from stock pot. Do not throw away the water.
3. Shred chicken, throwing away skin
4. Put shredded chicken in large bowl.
5. Add remaining ingredients
6. Pour some water from stock pot over mixture
7. Mix until pasty
8. Cover and refrigerate overnight

Dough:

Egg Noodle Dough (see recipe page 88)

Directions:

1. Roll dough out until paper thin

2. Put teaspoonfuls of filling in a row (see filling recipe below)

3. Fold over dough and cut with ravioli cutter

4. Seal edges with fork

5. Add to boiling water

6. They are done when they float to the top

7. They are done when they float to the top

8. Serve and enjoy!

Chicken Kabobs and Vegetable Kabobs

My family made this for 4th of July for dinner. We made two types of kabobs so we could have more options. These are nice and smokey from being on the grill outside and also the meat is extremely tender. These can be put together in advance and grilled the next day but it is a lot better to do it the same day.

Ingredients:

    4 boneless, skinless chicken breasts

    3 bell peppers

    2 pints of button mushrooms, whole

    2 medium white onions, cut

    soy sauce

    salt

pepper

onion powder

garlic powder

Directions:

1. Marinade the cubes of chicken in soy sauce, salt, pepper, onion powder, and garlic powder in a large bowl for about a couple hours

2. After you soak the skewers, add a mushroom then chicken, then pepper, then chicken, then onion, and the chicken and repeat until all the veggies and chicken are gone

3. Put them on the grill 10 minutes on each side or until done

4. For the vegetable kabobs, add the vegetables in any order you like and cook them just like the chicken kabobs

5. Serve and enjoy

Chicken Pinwheels

This is a recipe that I helped my mom with for lunch one day. This recipe is so delicious and moist because of the mayonnaise I used. This recipe is so good that I even ate it even though I am not a chicken-lover.

Ingredients:

4 boneless,skinless chicken breasts

6 ounces broccoli, steamed and mashed

spoonful of butter

salt, to taste

pepper to taste

parmesan cheese

1 ½ cups mayonnaise

2 cups regular breadcrumbs

Directions:

1. Take the chicken breasts and pound them out as best you can
2. Steam the broccoli until soft and then mash the broccoli
3. Take a little bit of butter and put it in the middle of the chicken breasts
4. Add a little bit of broccoli to each breast
5. Add a little parmesan cheese to each chicken breast. Then add salt and pepper
6. Roll the chicken breasts and seal with toothpicks
7. Roll in mayonnaise and breadcrumbs
8. Cook chicken at 375 degrees for 45 minutes
9. Remove from oven and let cool
10. Remove toothpicks
11. Serve and enjoy!

Deep Fried Smoked Salmon and Cream Cheese Wontons

I came up with this recipe because I love smoked salmon. This recipe can be made for parties or just a family dinner. This dish is so creamy and so delicious that when you eat it you feel like you are in heaven. You can also double the recipe if you have a lot of people over.

Ingredients:

½ pound of smoked salmon

½ cup Philadelphia cream cheese

1 4 oz container goat's milk feta cheese

1 4 oz block mild goat cheese

2 tablespoons whole grain mustard

6 wonton wrappers

¼ teaspoon ground red pepper

1 teaspoon black pepper

½ teaspoon kosher salt

1 tablespoon minced garlic

1 teaspoon onion powder

Directions:

1. Mix the salmon, cream cheese, feta cheese, goat cheese, mustard, red pepper, black pepper, salt, and minced garlic in a medium sized bowl.
2. Take the wonton wrappers and fill each one with a big spoon full of the filling.
3. Smear a little water on all sides of the wontons with your finger.
4. Fold the wonton over and pinch the front closed.
5. Fold the sides up as well. Put a little water on both sides first.
6. Fry in a shallow pan in about a couple inches of vegetable oil until golden brown on all sides.
7. Remove from oil and put on a plate lined with paper towel.
8. Serve with sour cream and enjoy!

Gianna's Shrimp Alfredo

This recipe is something I came up with on my own. Instead of using fettuccine I used linguine. I even made the Alfredo sauce from scratch adding my own spices of ground red pepper and cayenne pepper. This recipe can be used with fresh shrimp or frozen shrimp. I suggest you use fresh if you can. Also, if the sauce is too thin, you can use some flour to thicken it up.

Ingredients:

Alfredo Sauce:

    1/8 cup fresh parsley, chopped

    2 cups heavy cream

    1 cup milk

    2 teaspoons salt

    2 teaspoons pepper

    3 teaspoons cayenne pepper

3 teaspoons ground red pepper

1 bag frozen shrimp, thawed

1 ½ cups grated parmesan cheese

2 handfuls flour

¼ cup butter, melted

linguine pasta (any brand)

Directions:

1. Melt the butter in a medium saucepan on medium low heat. Add cream and milk and simmer for 5 minutes. Add cheese, parsley, and seasonings. Stir quickly.
2. Add the shrimp to the sauce and stir
3. Mix the sauce with the cooked pasta
4. Serve and enjoy!

Gouda-Stuffed Hamburgers

I decided to make this recipe because I love hamburgers. This recipe is gooey and delicious. This recipe is perfect for parties or just as a regular dinner. Remember, you have to pack these tightly or they will fall apart (which is exactly what happened to my burgers).

Ingredients:

1 pound ground chuck

1/8 teaspoon garlic powder

2 pinches salt

1 teaspoon black pepper

1 tablespoon yellow mustard

1 teaspoon minced garlic

1 teaspoon horseradish

1 egg

1 cup breadcrumbs

½ small container crumbled blue cheese

6 slices gouda cheese

Directions:

1. Mix the ground chuck, garlic powder, salt, pepper, mustard, minced garlic, horseradish, egg, and breadcrumbs in a small bowl.
2. Take some of the meat mixture and flatten it out.
3. Put 2 slices of cheese in the middle and put more meat on the top. Seal well.
4. Repeat this process.
5. Lay on a cookie sheet that is lined with aluminum foil and sprayed.
6. Cook in a 400 degree oven for 10 minutes on one side. Flip and cook for another 15 minutes on the other side.
7. Remove from oven and let cool.
8. Serve on a bun with your choice of toppings and enjoy!

Italian Stuffed Red Peppers

This is a recipe that I made with my dad for dinner one night. This recipe is very delicious and healthy (sort of). This is a perfect recipe for like a family dinner or a party. This recipe has rice in it so it resembles a porcupine. This also has Italian sausage and ground beef so it is very meaty. This recipe can be done in advance or on the same day you serve it for a meal. If you have a big party you can always make more. You can also serve this with mashed potatoes.

Ingredients:

½ pound ground beef

1 pound Italian sausage

1 egg

1 packet onion soup mix

1 teaspoon garlic powder

1 teaspoon dried basil

5 red bell peppers

mozzarella cheese

6 large white button mushrooms, chopped

1 bag of jasmine rice

Directions:

1. Take the bell peppers and cut the tops off and take all the membranes and seeds out.
2. In a medium-sized bowl, mix the beef, Italian sausage, egg, onion soup mix, garlic powder, dried basil, mushrooms, and rice very well.
3. Stuff each pepper with a big handful of the beef mixture.
4. Put in a glass baking dish (9x13) and cover with foil.
5. Bake in a 375 degree oven for 2 hours.
6. When the peppers are almost done cooking, take them out and take off the foil and add a big handful of mozzarella cheese.
7. Put it back in the oven to melt the cheese.
8. Remove from oven and let cool.
9. Serve and enjoy!

Loaded Chicken and Potatoes

My dad found this recipe on the internet and decided to make it for lunch. I helped him with this dish and it turned out to be really good. I decided to add sweet Italian sausage to the dish. This dish is very hearty and delicious. This can be made for a small dinner or a big holiday feast. This recipe can be made the day before in advance. This recipe called for hot sauce but I did not use it at all.

Ingredients:

1 pound cooked or raw boneless chicken breasts, cubed (1")

6-8 skin on red potatoes, cut in ½" cubes

1/3 cup olive oil

1 teaspoon black pepper

2 tablespoons garlic powder

hot sauce(optional)

½ pound bacon, cut

onion powder, to taste

1 ½ pounds sweet Italian sausage

2 cups fiesta cheese blend

1 cup diced green onions

Directions:

1. Preheat oven to 400 degrees. Spray a 9"x13" baking dish with cooking spray.
2. In a large bowl mix together the olive oil, salt, pepper, onion powder, garlic powder. Mix the sausage and potatoes in a small bowl and add the other ingredients. place that in the dish with the chicken.
3. Bake for about 55-60 minutes until the potatoes and sausage are cooked through.
4. Remove dish from the oven and add the cheese, bacon(chop and cooked first), and green onions on top.
5. Put the dish back in the oven for 5-10 minutes until the cheese is melted
6. Serve with sour cream and more hot sauce and enjoy!

Nutty Korean Chicken Tenders

This recipe was a something that my dad and I came up with because we both love chicken tenders and we wanted to try something different. We also used nuts to coat the chicken to give it a nice nutty flavor. These chicken tenders also have a garlicky flavor to counteract the tangy taste of the Korean barbeque sauce.

Ingredients:

1 pound boneless, skinless chicken breasts (½ inch strips)

½ a bottle of Korean barbecue sauce

2 ½ tablespoons minced garlic

1 tablespoon onion powder

½ teaspoon salt

½ teaspoon pepper

cashews

Directions

1. Gather the ingredients
2. Put the chicken into a medium bowl
3. Add the barbecue sauce, garlic, onion powder, salt, and pepper
4. Let marinade overnight in refrigerator
5. Pan-fry the chicken in a skillet until thoroughly cooked
6. Let cool
7. Eat and enjoy!

Oyster and Clam Chowder

I came up with this recipe because I wanted to make a chowder that was completely different from any other chowder. This recipe is very creamy and delicious because I put grated Parmesan cheese and half and half cream. This recipe takes a little while to make but be patient. It is worth it because it is so phenomenal. If you are having a big party, you can double the recipe.

Ingredients:

2 small red potatoes, diced

¾ cup all-purpose flour

3 cups half and half

1 can whole clams with the juice

1 can whole oysters with juice

5 slabs bacon, cooked

1 teaspoon dill weed

½ teaspoon salt

1 teaspoon black pepper

1 teaspoon parsley

1 cup grated parmesan cheese

2 tablespoons green onion, snipped

1 small onion, diced

Directions:

1. In a pot, melt the butter on medium heat.
2. Add the onions and cook until clear.
3. Stir in the flour. Cook for 2-4 minutes while stirring frequently.
4. Add the clams and oysters including the juice. Bring to a boil. Reduce heat and simmer for 15 minutes.
5. In a separate pot add the potatoes to some boiling water. Boil for about 15 minutes.
6. Add the potatoes to the other pot. Slowly add the half and half, dill, salt, pepper, parsley, Parmesan cheese, bacon, and green onions.
7. Heat through but do boil. Serve with saltine crackers or oyster crackers and enjoy!

Roasted Red Pepper and Goat Cheese Soup

This is a recipe that I made because I love bell peppers and I wanted to be different from everyone else. Originally this recipe would make 3 servings but it will make more in a bigger batch. This recipe is kind of spicy and also creamy from the heavy cream and milk . This recipe is so good. You can also serve this with Italian bread or crackers.

Ingredients:

4 red bell peppers, roasted, seeded, peeled, and cut

1 half pint container heavy whipping cream

1 small log mild goat cheese

1 1/3 cups low sodium chicken broth

5 garlic cloves, chopped

3-4 pinches kosher salt

3 teaspoons black pepper

½ teaspoon ground red pepper

4 teaspoons onion powder

½ of a large yellow onion, quartered and chopped

2 splashes balsamic vinegar

3 tablespoons fresh basil, washed and torn

1 tablespoon fresh Italian or plain parsley, washed and torn

3 splashes milk

Directions:

1. Wash and roast 4 red bell peppers in the oven at 425 degrees for 21 minutes until soft.
2. Peel the skin of with the tongs.
3. Cut into large pieces and place in blender omitting the stems.
4. Blend until very smooth.
5. Add a splash of the heavy cream, some chicken broth, the garlic, most of the onion, and ½ the amount of all the seasonings and herbs including some of the vinegar.
6. Blend well.
7. Add to a small pot and simmer on low heat.
8. Add the cheese, some more broth, and other half of the seasonings including some more balsamic.

9. Stir and simmer until kinda thick. Add the milk and stir

10. Turn of the heat and let cool

11. Serve in bowls and garnish with more torn basil

12. Enjoy!

Spicy Shrimp Salad

I decided to make this dish because I love shrimp salad. This recipe has my own unique ingredient in it and that is mascarpone cheese. This recipe can be made ahead of time and put in the refrigerator for the next day or you can make it the same day and have it fresh. This is the perfect side dish for like a steak or something.

Ingredients:

1 pound of cooked shrimp

1 cup mascarpone cheese

2 tablespoons dijon mustard

1 cup mayonnaise

1 tablespoon dill, chopped

1 tablespoon parsley, chopped

1 teaspoon black pepper

1 teaspoon salt

1 ½ tablespoons minced garlic

½ teaspoon red pepper flakes

Directions:

1. Mix the shrimp, mascarpone cheese, dijon mustard, mayonnaise, dill, parsley, black pepper, salt, minced garlic, and red pepper flakes in a medium bowl.
2. Refrigerate until ready to serve.
3. Enjoy!

Spicy Baked Scottish Eggs

This recipe for Scottish eggs is unique because I decided that I wanted to make them spicy. Also, this recipe is great for any main meal because they are ginormous in size. These eggs are packed with flavor from the bacon and the bratwurst sausage. This can be made in advance and put in the refrigerator for the next night to cook.

Ingredients:

2 bratwurst sausages

5 eggs, boiled and peeled

4 slabs of bacon

1/2 cup oatmeal

½ cup traditional breadcrumbs

1 tablespoon hot sauce

½ tablespoon prepared horseradish

1 teaspoon salt

½ teaspoon black pepper

1 tablespoon low sodium soy sauce

1 teaspoon onion powder

Directions:

1. Ground up the oatmeal in the food processor.
2. Remove the sausage from the casing and put in a large bowl. Tear the bacon into small pieces and add to sausage. Add the oatmeal and breadcrumbs to the meat.
3. Add the salt, pepper, onion powder, soy sauce, horseradish, hot sauce, and one egg to the meat. Mix well.
4. Add the 4 remaining eggs to a pot of water and bring to boil. Cover with lid.
5. Remove eggs from water and peel.
6. Take a big handful of meat and flatten it on the plate. Add the egg in the middle and fold meat around it(add more if needed).
7. Repeat.
8. Bake in a 375 degree oven for 45 minutes(30 minutes on bottom rack and 15 minutes on top rack).
9. Remove from oven and let cool
10. Serve with ant dipping sauce
11. Enjoy!

Spinach, Ricotta, and Shrimp Lasagna

This recipe is one that I came up with on my own because I love cheese, seafood, and spinach so I decided to make a mini lasagna. You can either make a big lasagna or individual mini lasagnas. This recipe can be made in advance for any occasion and it can be frozen or refrigerated. This recipe is absolutely to die for because it is so good.

Ingredients:

Egg Noodle Dough(see recipe below)

Egg Noodle Dough

> *Ingredients*:
>
> > 6-12 eggs (depending on how much dough you want)
> >
> > 4-8 cups all-purpose flour(or until it is the consistency you want)
> >
> > ¼ cup of salt

Directions:

1. Gather ingredients
2. Mix ingredients in medium bowl
3. Knead the dough
4. Place the dough in an oiled pan and let rise foe two hours

Pepper Marinara(see recipe page 44)

1 cup ricotta cheese

½ cup frozen shrimp, thawed and cut in half

1 cup fresh spinach, rinsed and torn into pieces

shredded mozzarella cheese (for topping)

Directions:

1. Roll out the dough and use a class to cut out small circles(cut out about 8 circles
2. Mix the shrimp, spinach, and ricotta cheese in large bowl
3. Place one circle on the bottom of the muffin tin
4. Put about a tablespoon of filling and a tablespoon of sauce on top of each circle
5. top each one with a small handful of cheese and another tablespoon of sauce
6. Bake in a 350 degree oven for 30-40 minutes
7. Take out and let cool
8. Eat and enjoy!

Sweet Italian Sausage and Three Cheese Ravioli

I decided to make this because I love ravioli and wanted to try and make my own version. It takes awhile to make but trust me it is worth the hard work. This recipe is good for holidays or any other event. You can make the filling in advance a day earlier and make the dough and cook the ravioli the next day.

Ingredients:

Egg Noodle Dough (see page 86)

Filling:

1 pound sweet Italian sausage

½ teaspoon salt

1 teaspoon black pepper

2 teaspoons garlic powder

1 cup ricotta cheese

2 cups shredded mozzarella cheese

½ cup parmesan cheese

2 tablespoons minced garlic

Directions:

1. In a large bowl mix the flour, eggs, and salt until it turns doughy. Place in a bowl with oil, cover and let sit for 2 hours.
2. Remove from bowl and roll the dough out as thin as possible.
3. Put about a tablespoon of filling about an inch apart. Fold the dough over the filling.
4. Cut out each individual ravioli with a small pizza cutter.
5. Cook the pasta in boiling water in a large pot.
6. Drain the pasta.
7. Serve with salt, pepper, and Parmesan cheese or with alfredo sauce.
8. Enjoy!

The Daddy Delight

This is a recipe I came up with for my dad for an early Father's Day present. I made this for my dad because he likes Asian food so I stuffed the steak with Asian ingredients. This recipe is special to me because it reminds me of my dad.

Ingredients:

1 tablespoon black pepper

2 cups chopped, cooked shrimp

½ cup green onion, cut

2 eggs, scrambled

1 cup Korean barbeque sauce

1 teaspoon rosemary leaves

1 teaspoon smoked paprika

1 teaspoon salt

1 round steak

½ cup all-purpose flour

1/8 cup parmesan cheese

Directions:

1. Mix shrimp, onions, and barbeque sauce in a medium bowl.
2. Scramble the eggs
3. Add the eggs to the pounded steak then add shrimp
4. Roll the steak and close with toothpicks
5. Roll in flour and parmesan mixture
6. Pan-fry it for about 5 minutes
7. Place in the oven for an hour
8. Remove from oven and let it rest
9. Carve and serve with extra barbeque sauce

White Pizza with Spicy Capi Cola, Green peppers, Mozzarella, and Black Olives

I made this recipe because I wanted to do something different with an Italian classic. This recipe is made from scratch which makes it all the more better. This makes a perfect family dinner entree or a great holiday dinner. This pizza is delicious and easy to make.

Ingredients:

1 cup water

1 yeast packet

4 cups flour

¼ cup olive oil

1 teaspoon salt

1 teaspoon sugar

1 teaspoon dried oregano

½ cup grated parmesan cheese

4-5 slices spicy capi cola

1 green bell pepper, chopped

½ can black olives

mozzarella cheese, shredded

Alfredo Sauce(see recipe page 68)

Directions:

1. Mix the flour, oil, salt, sugar, oregano, Parmesan cheese, and yeast in a large bowl. Activate the yeast in the water first using a coffee cup.
2. When it gets to a doughy consistency knead it with your hands.
3. Let the dough rise for two hours.
4. After the dough rises, roll it out on the table.
5. Add the Alfredo sauce, capi cola, olives, green peppers, and cheese(add as much as you like).
6. Bake the pizza in a 400 degree oven for 20 minutes.
7. Remove from oven and let cool.
8. Serve and enjoy!

Side Dishes

Cucumber Salad

This cucumber salad is a delicious accompaniment to my family's ribs, kabobs, and deviled eggs. This recipe is so delicious and easy to make. You can make it for a holiday like 4th of July(like we did) or just on a normal, uneventful day. This dish is able to be made the night before and served the next day.

Ingredients:

3 large cucumbers, thinly sliced

1 large onion, cut

1 cup white vinegar

½ cup white sugar

salt to taste

pepper to taste

dill to taste

Directions:

1. Mix the cucumber,onion,vinegar,sugar,salt,pepper,and dill in a bowl

2. Put in refrigerator until ready to serve

3. Serve, eat, and enjoy

Garlic and Shrimp Twice-Baked Potatoes

I made this recipe because I wanted to make my own version of baked potatoes. This recipe is very simple to make and it can be made in advance. Remember, if you have a latex allergy, you cannot handle raw potatoes so please use a sous chef. This recipe is so delicious. It is a perfect side dish for a steak or pork chop.

Ingredients:

3 garlic cloves, chopped

2 cans mini shrimp, drained

1 teaspoon salt

1 teaspoon black pepper

3 baking potatoes

shredded mozzarella, for topping

2 tablespoons green onions, chopped

1 tablespoon chives, chopped

2 tablespoons butter

1 cup milk

½ teaspoon red pepper flakes

2 tablespoons crumbled blue cheese

Directions:

1. Put the potatoes in the microwave for 5 minutes to partially cook them. Poke holes in the potatoes first.
2. Hollow out the potatoes with a spoon and put it into a bowl. Cut in half first.
3. Mix in the green onions, chives, garlic, shrimp, salt, pepper, red pepper flakes, butter, milk, blue cheese in with the potatoes.
4. Put some of the filling into each half and top with mozzarella cheese.
5. Put the potatoes into the broiler for 5-7 minutes until cheese is melted.
6. Remove from oven and let cool.
7. Serve and enjoy!

Potato Salad

This recipe is a dish that my family made for 4th of July. It is so delicious and simple to make. It is creamy from the mayonnaise and crunchy from the celery. This salad can be made in advance the night before and warmed and served the next day. If you want you can add some other ingredients to make it your own.

Ingredients:

9 medium potatoes, peeled and cubed

3 stalks celery

7 eggs,boiled

salt to taste

pepper to taste

2 teaspoons dill

smoked paprika to taste

2 tablespoons yellow mustard

½ cup mayonnaise (you can add more if needed)

Directions:

1. Wash, peel, and cube the potatoes
2. Put into a stockpot and cover with water
3. Bring potatoes to a boil
4. Turn down to a simmer for 15 minutes
5. Remove potatoes from stove, drain, and let cool
6. Dice celery stalks
7. Add to the bowl of potatoes
8. Chop four eggs and add to bowl
9. Save remaining eggs
10. Add salt, pepper, dill, mustard, and mayonnaise
11. Mix thoroughly
12. Slice remaining boiled eggs
13. Lay on top of potato salad
14. Refrigerate until ready to serve

Sweet Potato Fries

I came up with this recipe because I love sweet potatoes. I also made this to accommodate people with latex allergies. People with this allergy cannot handle raw regular potatoes but they can handle raw sweet potatoes (I do not know why). I made these salty, garlicky, and kinda sweet. This recipe is so dang good. If you are cooking for a large group you can double the recipe.

Ingredients:

1 large sweet potato

4 handfuls all-purpose flour

2 1/2 teaspoons garlic powder

olive oil spray

1 ½ teaspoons salt

1 tablespoon rosemary leaves

2 tablespoons black pepper

2 teaspoons smoked paprika

½ teaspoon ground nutmeg

olive oil (for frying)

Directions:

1. Peel the potato
2. Cut the potato in wedges as big or small as you want
3. Mix the flour, garlic powder, salt, pepper, rosemary, paprika, and nutmeg on a plate
4. Dredge the fries in the flour mixture
5. Fry in batches in a medium pan with about an inch of olive oil on medium to high heat
6. Lay on a plate lined with a paper towel to drain
7. Serve with my ketchup recipe (see above)
8. Eat and enjoy!

Tomato-Free Baked Beans

These beans are not like your typical baked beans because I made a tomato-free ketchup to go inside of the dish because I cannot have regular ketchup. These beans are so delicious that you will not even miss the typical tomato ketchup.

Ingredients:

4 cans of navy beans, drained

¾ cup Tomato-Free Ketchup (see recipe page 11)

2-3 handfuls brown sugar

1 tablespoon yellow mustard

pepper, to taste

2-3 slabs of bacon

1 medium white onion

½ cup real maple syrup

Directions:

1. Drain the beans and wash them in the sink (use a strainer)
2. Saute the onions and the bacon in a pan until translucent
3. Mix the beans, bacon and onion mixture, ketchup, brown sugar, mustard, pepper, and maple syrup
4. Place beans in a pan and cook in the oven for an hour at 375 degrees
5. Remove from the oven and let cool
6. Enjoy!

Desserts

Mini Blueberry Shortcakes

This recipe is one that my dad made for me on Memorial Day. He made this for me because I cannot have strawberries and he originally made strawberry shortcakes. This recipe was so good that I almost felt like I was going to go in a sugar coma! This recipe is nice and sweet and delicious, thanks to my father.

Ingredients:

A package of mini store-brought shortcakes

1/3 cup white sugar

2-3 cup blueberries(you can slice or mash them to allow the juices to come out)

Cool-Whip (for the top)

Directions:

1. Gather the ingredients
2. Mix the blueberries and sugar in a bowl and place in refrigerator for a couple hours to let the juices flow out
3. Take the shortcakes and place the blueberries(about a spoonful or two)that were in the refrigerator in the middle
4. Top with cool-whip and more blueberries
5. Eat and enjoy!

Peanutty Chocolaty Pies

I came up with this recipe to combine the sweet ingredients that I love. I had this amazing idea to use peanut butter and white chocolate. This is a recipe that you can pick up with your hands and eat without getting messy. You can add some more ingredients to put your creative spin on it if you desire.

Ingredients:

½ cup graham crackers, crushed by hand

½(8oz) pack cream cheese

½ bag of white chocolate chips, melted

cashews

½ stick butter, melted

¼ cup creamy peanut butter

Directions:

1. Gather the graham crackers, chocolate, cream cheese, cashews, butter, silicone muffin tins(or whatever you can find), and the food processor
2. Mix the graham crackers and melted butter in the food processor until well blended
3. Melt the white chocolate in the microwave on ½ power about 2 minutes, stirring every 30 seconds
4. Mix the cream cheese and peanut butter in a small bowl and then put it in the microwave for 30 seconds on ½ power
5. Place about a tablespoon of the crust on the bottom of each muffin tin
6. Put the same amount of the peanut butter and cream cheese mixture on top
7. Place some cashews on top of the mixture
8. Add a tablespoon of the white chocolate on top
9. Place more cashews on top
10. Place in the fridge about 1 hour
11. Remove from the fridge
12. Eat and enjoy!

Spicy Chocolate Cupcakes with Chocolate Cream Cheese Frosting

I came up with this recipe because I wanted to make my own play on cupcakes, which are my favorite dessert. This recipe is kind of spicy because of the cayenne pepper. This recipe is so moist and so delicious that when you eat it you feel like you are in heaven. You can also use confectioner's sugar.

Ingredients:

Cupcakes:

1 1/3 cups all-purpose flour

¼ teaspoon baking soda

2 teaspoons baking powder

¾ teaspoon cocoa powder

1 teaspoon salt

3 tablespoons butter, softened

1 ½ cups white sugar

2 eggs

1 cup milk

¾ teaspoon vanilla creamer or vanilla extract

1 tablespoon brewed coffee (any brand is fine)

2 1/8 teaspoon cayenne pepper

Frosting:

1/3 cup milk

1/3 cup all-purpose flour

1/3 cup vegetable shortening

1/3 cup butter, softened

1 2/3 cups confectioner's sugar

1/3 teaspoon vanilla creamer or vanilla extract

1/3 cup chocolate syrup

1/3 cup cream cheese

1 tablespoon brewed coffee

Directions:

1. Sift the dry ingredients into a large bowl. Add the wet ingredients into the dry ingredients and mix with an electric mixer on medium speed.
2. Take the cupcake tins and put one cupcake liner in each one.
3. Fill the tins ¾ of the way with batter.
4. Bake in a 350 degree oven for 22 minutes.
5. Remove from oven and let cool.
6. Mix the milk, flour, shortening, butter, sugar, vanilla creamer, chocolate syrup, cream cheese, and coffee in a medium bowl.
7. Pipe or spoon about a Tablespoon of the frosting onto each cupcake.
8. Serve and enjoy!

Refrigerator Cake

I made this recipe with my dad one day and I decided to use it for this cookbook. This cake is very simple to make, but it is very delicious. I do not know why this is called a refrigerator cake, but that is what its called so I just went with that name. This cake can be used for a birthday cake or just a dessert for an uneventful day.

Ingredients:

Cake: 2 boxes sugar-free yellow cake mix

    6 eggs

    2 cups water

    2/3 cup vegetable oil

    2 packs lime gelatin

Frosting: 1 tub Cool Whip (small tub)

2 packs instant lemon jell-o pudding

Directions

1. Put cake mix into a large bowl

2. Add 6 eggs

3. Add 2 cups water

4. Add 2/3 cup of vegetable oil

5. Mix with mixer on medium speed for two minutes

6. Grease a 9x12 rectangular pan with butter

7. Bake at 325 degrees for 34-38 minutes

8. Remove from oven

9. Stick toothpick in to see if the cake is done

10. Pour the gelatin mix in bowl

11. Follow directions on box to make the gelatin

12. Pour gelatin all over cake

13. Get a small bowl

14. Follow directions on box to make the pudding

15. Spread the pudding all over the cake

16. Cut and enjoy!

Vegan Peanut Butter and Nut Balls

I wanted to make this recipe for a friend of mine who is a vegan. Even though I am not a vegan I wanted to try this out. This recipe is sweet from the honey and creamy from the peanut butter. I fell in love with this the first time I made it. This is good for holidays or just a dessert after dinner. This recipe is to die for because it is so good. This is very simple.

Ingredients:

1 cup chunky peanut butter

1 cup cashews, salted

3 tablespoons honey

1 tablespoon sugar

1 cup butterscotch chips

1 ½ cups all-purpose flour

Directions:

1. Mix the flour, sugar, peanut butter, honey, cashews, and butterscotch chips in a small bowl.
2. Form into small balls and squeeze tightly. Roll some in sugar ad leave some plain.
3. Place on a cookie sheet lined with aluminum foil that is sprayed.
4. Cook in a 350 degree oven for 12 minutes.
5. Remove from oven and let cool.
6. Serve with caramel or powdered sugar.
7. Enjoy!

White Chocolate Peanut Butter Fudge

This recipe for White Chocolate Peanut Butter Fudge is so rich and flavorful. It is a great alternative for people who do not eat other types of chocolate. If you want, you can ad crushed pretzels to this to make it more crunchy.

Ingredients:

2 (14 ounce) cans Eagle Brand Sweetened Condensed milk

1 cup Jiffy creamy peanut butter

2 (12 ounce) packages white chocolate chips (you can use either squares or bars as well)

1 2/4 cups chopped nuts (any nut will work for this recipe)

2 teaspoons vanilla extract

Directions:

1. In a heavy saucepan, heat sweetened condensed milk and peanut butter over medium heat until just bubbly, stirring constantly.

2. Remove pan from heat. Stir in white chocolate until smooth. Immediately stir in peanuts and vanilla.

3. Spread mixture evenly into wax paper lined 8-or 9-inch pan. Cool. Cover and chill 2 hours or until firm.

4. Turn fudge onto cutting board; peel off paper. Sprinkle with additional chopped peanuts if desired. Cut into squares. Store leftovers covered in refrigerator.

Signature Burgers

The Big Daddy Burger

I decided to make this burger for my dad because I wanted to make something that best describes him. This burger has some of his favorite flavors inside. My dad loves Asian food, so I decided to put a little soy sauce inside. This burger is a really good description of my beloved father.

Ingredients:

½ pound ground beef (80/20 blend)

½ teaspoon salt

½ tablespoon low sodium soy sauce

1 teaspoon black pepper

1 teaspoon dill

1 tablespoon minced garlic

1 tablespoon dijon mustard

5-6 slices aged cheddar cheese

pepperoni slices

Directions:

1. Mix the beef, salt, soy sauce, pepper, dill, garlic, and mustard in a medium-sized bowl.
2. Form into 1 inch patties. Pack the patties tightly.
3. Cook in a pan with a little olive oil on medium heat for 2-3 minutes on each side.
4. Remove the patties from the pan and place on a plate lined with paper towel. Before you remove the patties place a slice of cheddar on there and let it melt.
5. Serve on a bun with a slice of cheddar and a couple pieces of pepperoni.
6. Enjoy!

The Gianna Surprise

I made this burger as my own signature burger. This burger has some of my favorite flavors that best describes me. This was the first time I made burgers all by myself, so I was a little nervous but it turned out fine.

Ingredients:

1 pound ground beef

1 teaspoon low sodium soy sauce

1 teaspoon black pepper

2 tablespoons french fried onions

2 splashes Hoisin sauce

1/8 teaspoon cayenne pepper

1 tablespoon wasabi sauce

1 tablespoon clover honey

1 tablespoon yellow mustard

1 hamburger bun

Honey Mustard Sauce (see page 124)

shredded mozzarella

Directions:

1. Mix the beef, soy sauce, black pepper, french fried onions, Hoisin sauce, cayenne pepper, wasabi sauce, honey, and yellow mustard in a bowl.
2. Form into 1 inch patties. Pack tightly.
3. Cook in a pan with olive oil for about 3-4 minutes on each side on medium heat.
4. Add some shredded mozzarella cheese when the patty is in the pan.
5. Remove from pan and place on a plate lined with paper towels.
6. Serve on a bun with the honey mustard.
7. Enjoy!

The Grandma Dora Sandwich

I made this sandwich in dedication to my Grandma Dora. This sandwich has my grandma's favorite foods on it. My grandmother passed away many years ago even before I was born. She was Italian so I put roast beef, mozzarella cheese, and sweet relish on the sandwich. I actually did not have Italian bread so I used Texas toast instead, but if you have Italian bread, you can use that.

Ingredients:

4-5 slices roast beef

1 slice pepper jack cheese

1 slices Texas toast

1 tablespoon sweet relish

1 big handful mozzarella cheese

Directions:

1. Take the 2 slices of bread and put the roast beef on one end. Add the cheese and sweet relish. Put the second slice of toast on to the patty. Melt the cheese in the microwave or under the broiler.

2. Serve and enjoy!

The Grandpa Phil Burger

I made this burger in dedication to my grandpa who died in 2012. This burger has his favorite foods inside, especially green tea leafs. It also has pepper jack cheese to show that my grandpa was a feisty person. I also made a honey mustard sauce because that was what he loved.

Ingredients:

2 slices rye bread, toasted

1 pound ground beef

½ teaspoon salt

1 teaspoon black pepper

¼ teaspoon cayenne pepper

2 teaspoons green tea leafs, crushed

1 tablespoon clover honey

1 tablespoon yellow mustard

2 hard boiled eggs, peeled and chopped

1 egg

Honey Mustard Sauce:

    ½ cup yellow mustard

    ½ cup clover honey

    combine and mix

Directions:

1. In a bowl, mix the meat, salt, pepper, cayenne pepper, green tea leafs, clover honey, yellow mustard, and hard boiled eggs in a medium-sized bowl.
2. Form into patties that are ½ an inch thick. Pack tightly.
3. Cook in a medium-sized pan with olive oil until completely cooked through. About 3-4 minutes on each side. Add a slice of pepper jack cheese before removing the patties.
4. Remove from the pan and place on a plate lined with paper towel.
5. Serve on a bun with honey mustard sauce.
6. Enjoy!

The Momma Linda Burger

I made this burger as a signature burger for my mom, Linda West. This burger has some of her favorite flavors inside. This burger is kinda spicy because my mom loves spicy food. This burger was going to have coffee in it, but I decided not to do that.

Ingredients:

1 pound ground beef

½ teaspoon salt

1 teaspoon black pepper

½ tablespoon wasabi sauce

2 tablespoons French fried onions

1 tablespoon clover honey

1/8 teaspoon cayenne pepper

2 slices pepper jack cheese

1 hamburger bun

Directions:

1. Mix the ground beef, salt, pepper, wasabi sauce, French fried onions, honey, and cayenne in a medium-sized bowl
2. Form into one inch patties.
3. Cook in a medium-sized pan with olive oil for 3-4 minutes on each side. Put a slice of pepper jack cheese on each patty while they are still in the pan.
4. Remove and place the patties on a plate lined with paper towels.
5. Serve on a bun with honey mustard sauce on page 95.

The Rock Star Burger

I wanted to make a burger that best describes my brother, Ian. My brother loves music so that is what inspired the name of the burger. He also likes a little heat so I put a little red pepper flakes in the meat. This burger best describes my brother because he is a very simple laid back kid.

Ingredients:

½ pound ground beef (80/20 blend)

½ teaspoon salt

1/8 teaspoon red pepper flakes

1 teaspoon black pepper

1 tablespoon garlic powder

4-5 slices whole milk mozzarella cheese

3-4 slices of bacon

pepperoni

Directions:

1. Mix the beef, salt, black pepper, red pepper flakes, and garlic powder in a bowl.
2. Form into 1 inch patties and pack tightly.
3. Cook in a pan with olive oil on medium heat.
4. Add a piece of cheese o each patty and melt the cheese.
5. Remove the patties and place on a plate lined with paper towel.
6. Cook the bacon in the same pan until crispy.
7. Add a couple pieces of pepperoni.
8. Serve on a bun and enjoy!

Restaurant Reviews

The rating scale for my reviews would be on a scale from 1-5. 5 being perfect and 1 being not so great.

Field Stone Grill

On Thursday, May 16th 2013, I went to Field Stone Grill in Portage, Michigan. This restaurant looks like an upscale European restaurant that has good food and service. The food we had was really good. I had seared scallops with asparagus and saffron risotto and it was so good. It was the first time I had risotto and I love it now. The décor was very elegant. The service was great and the servers were very professional. It was worth the long drive from Illinois. The place was totally accessible even the bathrooms were accessible. I would absolutely go there again and I would give it five stars.

Five Guys Burgers and Fries

On Saturday November 30, 2013, I went to Five Guys Burgers and Fries with my dad. This place is a fast food joint whith burgers and fries that were voted the best around the country. The place is very clean and it is decorated with different signs with news articles that have voted the food as some of the best. The colors of the place are red, white and a little bit of black on the ceiling. I had a bacon and cheese hot dog with grilled onions and mushrooms and a cocoa cola drink and my dad had a hamburger and we shared Cajun spiced french fries. They were all very good. The staff is very friendly and professional. Also, when you first walk in, you can see the little kitchen and a lot of bags of peanuts. This place is definitely a good place to hang out with friends and family. I would definitely go back to this place. I would also give this place 5 stars.

Hibachi Restaurant and Grill

I went to Hibachi Restaurant and Grill in Matteson, IL with a few friends from a program I do. This restaurant is a Chinese buffet restaurant with a wide variety of delicious food . When I walked in, I noticed the restaurant was very family friendly and cozy. The food was very good and fresh. The employees were really nice and professional as well and I really liked that. I had sushi, zucchini, and other types of food and it was so good. It was a bit pricey but it was worth it. This restaurant was very accessible even though it was a bit crowded with people. It is so addicting so be careful not to eat to much like I did. I would definitely give this place a 5 because of the food, staff, decor, and accessibility.

Hyde Park Market Place

On Thursday, October 17 2013, I went to Hyde Park Market Place (located at the University of Chicago Hospital in Chicago, IL) with my mom. This place is a cafe and convenient store mixed into one. It has a warm feeling when you walk in because of the décor. It has a grass shade of green on the walls and there is a poster of Chicago that says eco-friendly. The entire cafe is very spacious because the tables are spread out. There are also trash cans for different types of trash which shows that the place recycles. The place has various cheeses and meats on the menu which are shown in little display cases. The place has a soup bar, salad bar, gelato bar, a hot bar, a dessert case, and some sushi on one side. On the other side there is a convenient store with drinks and snacks. The staff is very friendly. They hold open the door and help you carry your food to the table for you if you need help. I had a deluxe ham and cheddar sandwich and chicken noodle soup. They were both really good. I would definitely give this place 4 and a half stars and I would definitely go back.

Longhorn Steakhouse

I went to Longhorn Steakhouse in Orland Park, Illinois with my family to celebrate my parents' anniversary. I thought that the decor was very rustic with the horse bridles and the animal heads. I really liked the brown walls because brown is one of my favorite colors. I also liked how our server was so nice. I had the shrimp and lobster chowder and flounder stuffed with shrimp and lobster and it was so delicious. Our appetizers were phenomenal as well. I also really liked how the bathroom was handicapped accessible. I would give this restaurant a 5.

The one thing I would change would be the size of the tables because it was so crowded. I would also change the spacing of the tables because it was kind of crowded. I would definitely go back there again though.

Max and Benny's Restaurant, Bakery, and Deli

I went to Max and Benny's Restaurant, Bakery, and Deli in Northbrook, IL with my family. This restaurant was a family style restaurant that had light colors and it was very cozy and spacious. The staff was very friendly and professional. They were also very helpful. I ordered an adult grilled cheese and a matzoh ball soup and it was so good. The restaurant also had a big deli with a wide variety of food. It was a little pricey but it was worth it. It was also very wheelchair accessible even though the bathroom hallway was a little tight. I would definitely give it a 5. I would definitely go back there again.

MiMi's Cafe

On Sunday, March 17th 2013, my family and I went to MiMi's Cafe in Orland Park, IL. MiMi's is a French bistro with both American cuisine and French cuisine. The atmosphere is rustic and inviting. I had the quiche Lorraine with French onion soup and after that I had a chocolate mousse with strawberries and it was all delicious. The service was okay. The waitress was extremely nice, just a little forgetful. I would definitely go back there again and I would give it 4 ½ stars. The only thing I would change is the size of the tables because they were a bit too small.

Oma's Restaurant

On December 14th, 2013, my family and I went to Oma's Restaurant located in the Bavarian Inn Lodge in Frankenmuth, Michigan. We were staying at the lodge during Christmas break and it was wonderful. It is a cute German restaurant, decorated with several colors like green and a little red. The tables were nice and clean. The servers were extremely friendly, although they were kind of clueless on their soup of the day. I had weinersnitzel, which is German breaded veal, and it came with potato cakes and squash and it was really good. I also had a cup of cheddar ale soup and it was amazing. The accessibility was great and I was able to fit. I would definitely go back there again and I would give it 4 ½ stars. It was worth the drive from Illinois.

Cooking Challenges

One of my favorite things to do is cooking challenges with my dad. Let me explain what these cooking challenges are all about. My mom puts together a basket of different ingredients. My dad and I then go into the kitchen, open the basket and look at our ingredients. The dish can either be an appetizer, entree, or dessert. We have to base the dish on a specific theme that my mom gives us. We sometimes have a time limit but not all the time. After the dish is made, my mom then judges it on its flavor and creativity. Here is a sample:

Steve and G's Cooking Challenge

This cooking challenge will be an appetizer challenge. You may add whatever ingredients you like but you must use the following ingredients in some way:

Cool Whip

liver sausage

chicken

white chocolate

You must also give your appetizer a name that coincides with either 'marriage' or 'Epiphany'

You will have 30 minutes to complete the challenge.

Your time starts now. Good luck.

And this was the end result:

"Go, eat your food with gladness, and drink your wine with a joyful heart, for God has already approved what you do."

-Ecclesiastes 9:7

Made in the USA
Charleston, SC
05 October 2014